The FIRST BOOK of
AFRICA

The First Book of

AFRICA

by *Langston Hughes*

ILLUSTRATED WITH PHOTOGRAPHS

Franklin Watts, Inc.

575 Lexington Avenue • New York 22

Library of Congress Catalog Card Number: 59-5253

© COPYRIGHT 1960 BY FRANKLIN WATTS, INC.

Printed in the United States of America
by Polygraphic Company of America, Inc.

SECOND PRINTING

Contents

Unknown Africa

LONG after other continents were quite well known by the people of the world, Africa remained almost unexplored. Until the eighteenth century little but the fringes of the continent had been touched by outsiders. A hundred years ago, or a little more, large parts of Africa were still known as "darkest Africa," and they really were dark as far as knowledge of them went in other countries.

Why?

Murchison Falls, Uganda — one of Africa's many rapids

For one thing, the terribly hot, dry Sahara Desert in the north was a barrier to outsiders trying to reach Central Africa from that direction. Then, too, much of the African land away from the coast is a high plateau from which many rivers run in rocky rapids to the ocean; the boats of earlier days were not built to journey up such rivers. In addition, there were jungle thickets, strange wild animals, a frightening swarm of insects, an unfamiliar and often uncomfortable climate, tropical diseases, and unknown tribes that might be unfriendly.

North Africa was known because it could be reached by way of

Large-eared elephants, found wild only in Africa

the Mediterranean Sea. In many ways it was almost a part of Europe. But the Africa farther south — the Africa we are chiefly concerned with in this book — was little known until the past century. Then came a time of great exploration. Here are some of the things we know about Africa now.

Africa Today

OF the world's continents, Africa is second in size. It has an area of more than eleven millions of square miles and makes up about one-fifth of the land surface of the earth; it is bigger than the United States, India, and China put together. It has perhaps 224 millions of people; this is a guess, however, for not all its people have been counted. Not all its land has been explored, either, though its chief lakes and rivers are charted, and its mountains, deserts, and plains are properly shown on maps.

Its climate varies from temperate to tropical. The equator runs near the very middle of the continent. As a result, the heart of Africa has a tropical climate, hot, moist, and sunny except in the mountains, where some peaks have snow all the year round. In South Africa there is often snow in winter, but North Africa is temperate. If it were not for the warm waters of the Mediterranean Sea, however, winters in North Africa might be very cold.

Africa is one of the richest lands in the world. Most of the diamonds and almost half the gold on earth come from that continent. Uranium, copper, tin, iron, and other minerals of great value are found there, and so are cocoa beans, from which chocolate is made, rubber, coffee, cotton, palm oil, and ivory. Ebony, mahogany, and many other hardwoods are also products of Africa.

Because the continent is so rich in raw materials, Europeans set-

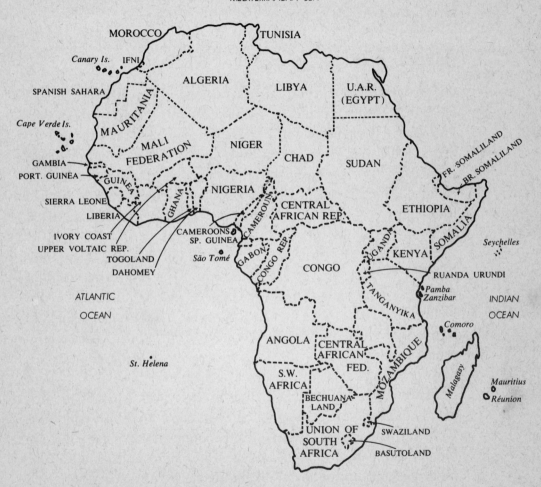

MEDITERRANEAN SEA

MOROCCO   TUNISIA

Canary Is. IFNI

ALGERIA   LIBYA   U.A.R.
(EGYPT)

SPANISH SAHARA

MAURITANIA

Cape Verde Is.

MALI
FEDERATION   NIGER   CHAD   SUDAN

GAMBIA
PORT. GUINEA

GUINEA

NIGERIA   CENTRAL
AFRICAN REP.   ETHIOPIA

SIERRA LEONE

LIBERIA

GHANA

FR. SOMALILAND
BR. SOMALILAND

SOMALIA   *Seychelles*

IVORY COAST

UPPER VOLTAIC REP.

CAMEROONS
SP. GUINEA

CAMEROUN

UGANDA   KENYA

TOGOLAND

DAHOMEY

São Tomé

GABON

CONGO REP.

CONGO

RUANDA URUNDI

TANGANYIKA

Pamba
Zanzibar

ATLANTIC

OCEAN

INDIAN

OCEAN

Comoro

ANGOLA   CENTRAL
AFRICAN
FED.   MOZAMBIQUE

St. Helena

S.W.
AFRICA

Malagasy   *Mauritius*
Réunion

BECHUANA-
LAND

UNION OF
SOUTH
AFRICA   SWAZILAND

BASUTOLAND

5

tled there long ago, and now control most of the area. They are white people. But in all of Africa there are only about five millions of such settlers, and more than half of them live at the very top or the very bottom of the continent — either in North Africa or in South Africa, where the climate is closest to that of Europe.

Most of the native peoples of Africa are black or dark brown, though some are lighter, and in the Arab countries of North Africa they may be tan or ivory white.

The greater number of the peoples of tropical Africa have their own tribal religions. They worship many varied gods. But about sixty million Africans are Moslems (also called Mohammedans) and about twenty-one million have been converted to Christianity. Most of the Moslems live in North Africa, and most of the Christians are in the coastal regions where European and American missionaries have been most active. There are also some African Jews, like the Falasha of Ethiopia.

Africa has many countries, which are grouped to make over forty political units. They have fascinating names, such as Tanganyika, Togoland, Nigeria, Senegal, Morocco, and Ethiopia. No two of the countries are alike, and they have many different tribes and different languages. More than seven hundred languages and dialects are spoken in Africa.

Before the coming of the Europeans, most of the African peoples had their own tribal governments, usually ruled by a chief who in many cases was advised by the elders of the tribe. Now the different countries have a variety of kinds of government. Some countries are completely independent, each with its own ruler, or with officials elected by the people. Some are self-governing members of the British Commonwealth. Others are colonies of a European power; they are under the protection of a European power; or they are watched over by the United Nations. England, France, Belgium, and Portugal control large areas of the African continent. But the aim of African peoples today is to be free of foreign management and to have the right to govern themselves.

Ancient Africa

AFRICA has had a long and fascinating history. Prehistoric skulls have recently been found in Kenya. They seem to show that more than a million years ago man may have had his beginnings on the African continent. Rock paintings of the Bushmen in South Africa seem to date from the early part of the Stone Age. And beautiful bronze heads discovered in Benin show that in ancient times people who were fine artists lived near the river Niger.

Rock paintings of the Bushmen

Bronze head of a girl, from Benin

Before the Golden Age of Greece or the rise of the Roman Empire both Ethiopia and Egypt had firmly established governments and standing armies. The people built great cities and carved enormous statues from stone. As early as 2600 B.C. the Egyptians had beautiful temples, tall pyramids, and handsome palaces. Herodotus, the "Father of History," recorded the splendor of the Pharaohs.

After a time, European peoples came into Egypt from across the Mediterranean, and others came from Asia. In the fourth century

Court of Rameses II, Luxor, Egypt (Moslem mosque in background)

9

B.C. the Greeks built schools there, and a thousand years later the Romans built roads. These invaders, as well as the Arabs, mixed with the Africans and produced along the Mediterranean a people with the many shades of skin coloring seen in Egypt today. In ancient times Egypt became the "crossroads of civilization."

The Egyptian kings were rich; many of them owned slaves. Some of the slaves were from the dark heart of Africa south of the Sahara, and at one time some were Jews or members of other captive groups. About three thousand years before Christ it became fashionable for wealthy Egyptians to own Pygmies, the little men from Central Africa who almost never grow more than four and one-half feet tall. Later, Homer speaks of Pygmies in his *Iliad*, as do Aristotle and the ancient Roman writer, Pliny, in their works. Apparently some knowledge of Africa has been recorded since the beginning of written history.

About 332 B.C., Alexander the Great added Egypt to his empire. He built there the city of Alexandria, which became a great center of learning and trade. Alexandria's lighthouse on the island of Pharos was one of the Seven Wonders of the Ancient World; and the city's library, later destroyed by Julius Caesar, contained thousands of books written on rolls of papyrus. Students from many parts of Africa and Asia visited Alexandria, and ships sailed from its port to all the world then known.

Long before Alexander's time, however, Phoenician sailors had explored the North African coastline, and Phoenician pioneers had founded the city of Carthage on what is now the shore of Tunisia. The Carthaginians, braving the vast, unknown waters of the Atlantic Ocean, ventured down the west coast of Africa as far south as Sierra Leone, but they did not go inland. The heart of equatorial Africa and all the region of the south remained unknown to outsiders for centuries until, early in 1488, the Portuguese rounded the Cape of Good Hope. Ten years later, on his way to India, Vasco da Gama visited the Kenya coast. Before the end of the Middle Ages trading had developed between Africa and Europe, and European ships were bringing home gold, olive oil, tropical fruits, nuts, and slaves. By then, as European explorers realized more fully the riches to be found in Africa, they were venturing ever farther up its rivers. But, hemmed in by the rivers and by mountains and jungles, and fearful of the natives, the explorers did not dare attempt many expeditions overland.

A camel driver in Villagio Abruzzi, Somalia

Great Kingdoms of Black Africa

LONG before Columbus discovered America, there had flourished in black Africa a number of large Negro kingdoms. The most remarkable were Ghana, Melle, and Songhay. By A.D. 300 the old state of Ghana stretched from Senegal southward to the sources of the Niger River. Its citizens worked farms, raised cattle, trapped elephants, and mined gold. Their largest city, Kumbi-Kumbi, was an important trading center. From the countries across the Sahara caravans came, laden with sugar, wheat, and cloth; they returned northward with gold, ivory, and rubber.

In 1067 a fierce fighting band of Moslems invaded Ghana and from then on its power grew less. Meanwhile, to the west, another Negro kingdom grew up, called Melle or Madingoland. It stretched from the Atlantic Ocean to Lake Chad, and within its borders were the rich gold mines of Bure. The rulers of Melle became so wealthy that in 1324, when King Gonga-Mussa, a Moslem, made a pilgrimage to Mecca, he took with him five hundred servants, each of whom carried on his head a slab of pure gold. In all, sixty thousand persons — soldiers, secretaries, camel drivers, and attendants — went with the king on his pilgrimage. Along the way he gave gifts freely to provincial governors, and ordered beautiful mosques built so that the distant towns of his realm might remember him. On his return from Mecca, King Gonga-Mussa brought with him an Arabian architect, Es Saheli, to help beautify the cities of Kangaba, Jenne, and Timbuktu.

Timbuktu was then a busy trading center, famous for its leatherwork, its white embroidered robes, its silks and pearls, perfume, ostrich plumes, dates, cloves, tea, and coffee. Timbuktu was also a center of learning, known for its libraries and bookstalls. To its

Reading lesson at a Moslem school in Nigeria

University of Sankoré came students and teachers from Cairo, Baghdad, and even as far away as Europe. From Sankoré professors carried their learning to other countries. One of the sheiks of Sankoré, Ahmed Baba, was a learned man, the author of some twenty books.

In 1469 the ruler of the kingdom of Songhay, Sunni Ali, sent his river navy down the Niger to capture the cities of Timbuktu and Jenne. Sunni Ali eventually gained control of all the land of Melle. By the beginning of the sixteenth century Songhay had become the most powerful state in West Africa. Under King Askia Mohammed, who was a great traveler, Songhay became friendly with surrounding states; new systems were set up for governing, trading, and banking; new schools were started. At the University of Sankoré the departments of surgery, law, and literature attracted students from the whole Moslem world. Until the Moors conquered Songhay in 1591 it was one of the most enlightened countries of its time, and in the Middle Ages the city of Timbuktu became one of the greatest centers of learning. But today it is only a drab West African town of about seven thousand inhabitants, at the end of a caravan route across the Sahara.

White Explorers

ALTHOUGH Portuguese seamen had sailed a short way up the Congo River in the late 1400's and by the 1600's had penetrated farther inland, and the Dutch had built a supply station for ships on the Cape of Good Hope in 1652, no large-scale European exploration into the heart of Africa began until the end of the eighteenth century. In 1795 Mungo Park, a Scottish traveler, was sent out from England by the African Association, a society whose purpose was to learn more about Africa. Park went up the Gambia River and later explored the Niger where it flows eastward before turning toward the south and west. In 1822 three Englishmen, Denham, Clapperton, and Oudney, began a historic crossing of the Sahara Desert. In 1851 David Livingstone discovered the Zambezi River, and a few years later reached Victoria Falls. In 1877 Henry Stanley traced the flow of the Congo. Wherever such Britishers went, others followed, claiming land for the English crown. At the same time explorers for other European powers were active.

Much of Britain's early interest in Africa came about through its part in the slave trade. To compete with the Dutch, the French, and the Portuguese in the ugly business of selling human beings, the King of England chartered the African Company in 1672. Thereafter England began to build forts and settlements along Africa's Atlantic seaboard. The other large European powers did the same thing. It was not long before almost the entire West African coast was under the power of Europeans who at the same time controlled all of North Africa and portions of the East Coast.

As early as 1575 the Portuguese took over the coast of what is now Angola. But Europeans were much longer in gaining control over the vast African interior, because of the lack of exploration, the difficulty of travel, and other drawbacks. The first white man, John Hanning Speke, did not go into Uganda until 1862. A few years before, he had discovered the source of the river Nile. In 1884 the Germans took over the Cameroons; in 1885 the Belgians began their rule of the Congo; and a little later the British South African Company began to gain control of Rhodesia and other inland territories in the queen's name. By the beginning of the twentieth century almost all of Africa belonged to Europe.

Livingstone and Stanley: Explorers

THE two greatest African explorers were David Livingstone and Henry Morton Stanley, both born in Great Britain. Livingstone was a missionary, and Stanley a newspaperman. Livingstone studied

Victoria Falls, Rhodesia

16

medicine at the University of Glasgow, and first set out for Africa a year before Stanley was born. Thirty years later their paths were to cross on that continent in a most dramatic way.

It was in 1840 that the London Missionary Society sent David Livingstone to Bechuanaland to pick places for the setting up of missions, to help convert the tribes to Christianity, and to see what could be done about stopping the slave trade. On his first trip Livingstone remained in Africa for nine years. In his travels he discovered Lake Ngami and the Zambezi River. On a second trip he followed the course of the Zambezi to the Indian Ocean and on the way discovered, in 1855, a mighty waterfall that he named after Queen Victoria. In 1858 he was made British consul to Quelimane. At the same time he continued his explorations.

Livingstone kept records and made maps of all his discoveries, and for the first time charted routes into the dark heart of Africa. He was past fifty when he organized an expedition to map the headwaters of the Nile. On this trip he disappeared into the Lake Tanganyika region and was not heard of for many months. His silence caused great anxiety among his friends. After more than two years the New York *Herald* sent its most famous reporter, Henry Stanley, in search of the famous missionary-explorer.

In his youth Stanley, an orphan, had shipped to New Orleans as a cabin boy. There he found a foster parent and remained in the United States. He served in the Confederate Army, and later in the United States Navy. Still later he became a foreign correspondent, making his first trip to Africa in 1867 to cover a British military invasion into Abyssinia.

In the spring of 1871 Stanley organized an expedition of 192 men to find Livingstone. They set out from Zanzibar and traveled by boat up rivers and on foot through jungles for more than six months before they located the aged missionary. On November 10, 1871, Livingstone was found in the village of Ujiji on the shores of Lake Tanganyika.

The first person to sight Dr. Livingstone was a native guide; he brought word to Stanley of a very old man with a very white beard. Stanley later wrote in his journal that at this news his heart began to beat very fast. He was so excited he wanted to turn handsprings and slash trees. But dignity would not allow such behavior. Instead, when he reached the village he walked with great ceremony through a throng of natives that surrounded the old missionary. Then, taking off his hat, he bowed and said quietly, "Dr. Livingstone, I presume?"

It was indeed Dr. Livingstone. Warmly he welcomed Stanley, and together they spent some four months. But Livingstone did not wish to be rescued. He wanted only to continue his explorations and his work as a missionary. After Henry Stanley left, Livingstone went farther into the jungle world and lived with the Africans. At the age of sixty he died on the shores of Lake Bangweulu, where his heart is buried beneath a tree. The natives wrapped his body in salt and carried it to Zanzibar. From there his remains were sent to London, to be buried in Westminster Abbey with other great men of English history.

In 1874 Stanley returned to Africa as an explorer in his own right. He became the first European to circle Lake Victoria and to chart its size as the second-largest fresh-water lake in the world. He was also the first white man to see Mount Ruwenzori, the Mountains of the Moon, and to travel by boat down the entire length of the Congo River. Riding the rapids on the Congo trip, his three white companions died before reaching the coast, and he lost two-thirds of his African carriers.

Stanley became famous for his explorations of the Congo, and he tried in vain to interest the British government in the riches he had found along the river's banks. He failed. Instead, King Leopold II of Belgium commissioned him to head an expedition into the Congo country. Within five years Stanley had set up the framework for complete Belgian control over the region, which was named the Congo Free State. Later, in England, Stanley was knighted for his contributions to the knowledge of Africa. As Sir Henry Morton Stanley he became a member of the British Parliament in 1895.

Both Stanley and Livingstone left behind them many books, records, and journals of their African discoveries. Stanley, in particular, wrote and lectured a great deal. But it was the missionary David Livingstone, rather than the more colorful and pushing Stanley, who expressed a modern feeling toward Africa and the values of exploration. Livingstone said that the exploration of a new country should be "a matter for congratulation *only* in so far as it opens up a prospect for the elevation of the inhabitants." If all European explorers and settlers had followed this noble belief, there might be no trouble in Africa today.

Cecil Rhodes: Empire Builder

EXPLORERS were not the only men fascinated by the almost unknown continent that was opening up. Pioneers like Cecil Rhodes soon learned that here they might find great wealth and power. Rhodes, the son of a minister, was born in England in 1853. As a youth he was frail, and for his health's sake doctors advised him to seek a warmer climate. At seventeen he set sail for South Africa; soon after he arrived he went into the Kimberley region to dig for diamonds. Two years later young Rhodes was a millionaire. At twenty-three he returned to England to enter the university at Oxford, but every year he went back to South Africa during his vacations, for Africa had become his home.

In addition to his diamond properties Rhodes soon had large interests in the mining of gold. Wealth gave him political power, and in 1881, the same year he received his degree from Oxford, he was elected to the Parliament of the Cape Colony. He was called an "unscrupulous land-grabber" by many, but Rhodes insisted that he had no interest in money for its own sake. His real aim was the advancement of the British Empire, he said, and his dream was that England should rule all of Africa, and in time, all the world. To this end he devoted his energies and his fortune.

In 1888 Rhodes founded De Beers Consolidated Mines, Ltd., which became one of the greatest mining combinations ever formed. At thirty-seven he was made Prime Minister of Cape Colony. He had already set up the British South Africa Company, which governed the area later named for him, the Rhodesias. He had also forced the annexation of Bechuanaland, and he bought from King Lobengula, king of the Matabele people, all the rights to search for minerals within an area of 75,000 square miles, for a payment of about $500 a month, 1,000 rifles, 100,000 rounds of ammunition, and the promise of an armed steamboat, which the king never received. Even Queen Victoria of England was shocked to hear of King Lobengula, especially when Rhodes employed a number of the king's sons as his servants. This "great empire builder" had little regard for the African people as he pushed British control northward from Cape Town almost to the Congo. Eventually he put some 800,000 square miles of land under English control.

"In Africa, think big," was one of his mottoes. He dreamed of a Cape-to-Cairo railroad to cross the length of the whole continent, and he brought about the building of long stretches of this railroad. It still is not finished. At Victoria Falls the line crosses one of the world's highest bridges, which allows passengers a view of one of the mightiest waterfalls on earth.

Rhodes was much against the Dutch government in the Transvaal, and his policies helped to bring about the Boer War in 1899. In this war the Dutch were defeated, and their colonies became a possession of Great Britain. The same year the war ended, Rhodes died and was buried in Rhodesia, the rich area of gold, copper, cobalt, zinc, and manganese that he had taken over for the English. In Rhodesia's meadows fat cattle graze; fertile fields grow wheat, corn, cotton, and tobacco. Across the grassy plains, leopards scream and lions roam. There, on a high, lonely hill that he himself had purchased for his tomb, Rhodes is buried; only by an act of Parliament may anyone else be laid to rest near him. He willed a part of his great fortune to Oxford University for the creation of the famous Rhodes scholarships, given annually to students of many nations.

Cecil Rhodes Memorial, Capetown, South Africa

Albert Schweitzer at the edge of the Ogowe River

Rhodes, Livingstone, and Stanley, all British, were the great pioneers in the opening up to Great Britain of Africa south of the equator. North of the equator, too, Britain had gained control in one way or another of enormous territories stretching south from the Mediterranean. At one time it was possible to map a route entirely on British-dominated territory from Cape Town northward across South Africa, through Bechuanaland and the Rhodesias into Tanganyika, Kenya, Uganda, then over the former Anglo-Egyptian Sudan through Egypt to Cairo near the northern coast — across the whole length of Africa.

Today Britain no longer has such power, although its holdings on the Dark Continent are still enormous and Africa is one of the great sources of its wealth. A sizable part of the wealth results from the efforts of Cecil Rhodes.

Albert Schweitzer: Missionary

ONE group of men and women who have had a tremendous influence on Africa have been neither explorers nor money-makers. They have been missionaries, both Protestant and Roman Catholic. The missionaries have been responsible for a good part of the education, hospitals, and health agencies that Africa now has. Almost the entire school system in the Belgian Congo is in the hands of hard-working monks and nuns of the Catholic faith. The most famous hospital on the continent, that of Dr. Albert Schweitzer at Lambaréné in jungle Africa, is a Protestant mission. It lies just north of the Congo River in the republic of Gabon. Founded by Dr. Schweitzer in 1913, it has become known around the world as a great center of tropical medicine.

Dr. Schweitzer has always been a scholar, and became first a Doctor of Philosophy at the University of Strasbourg, then a Doctor of Theology and the pastor of a church in Strasbourg. He was already an excellent organist, and later took a degree in music and became an authority on the music of Bach. At the age of thirty he decided to become a physician. For six years Albert Schweitzer studied medicine, and in 1911 was graduated as a medical doctor. Two years later he and his wife sailed for Africa as representatives of the Paris Missionary Society. He was then thirty-eight years old.

Dr. Schweitzer paid for all the first equipment for his hospital from his own earnings as a minister, public speaker, and organist. For its site he chose a lonely spot just south of the equator and almost two hundred miles from the African coast, because there a hospital was badly needed. The climate of Gabon is hot and humid. Leprosy is a common disease. Wild animals abound, and dangerous mosquitoes and the tsetse fly are widespread.

Except for brief returns to Europe, Dr. Schweitzer remained at Lambaréné for nearly fifty years. The story of his devotion to the saving of human lives in the heart of the African jungle is one of the great sagas of medical history. Albert Schweitzer himself has written a number of books. From them and from the many volumes that others have written about his work, the full story of this great man and his remarkable hospital may be learned. During his long life numerous honors have come his way, including a series of postage stamps bearing his picture and pictures of his hospital. Dr. Schweitzer received the 1952 Nobel Peace Prize for, in part, the belief he has often expressed that it is wrong "to regard the life of any living creature as worthless." His work and that of many other missionaries in both the medical and educational fields show what can be done to help Africa take her place in the modern world.

Albert Schweitzer's patients waiting their turn to be treated

Turkhana women of the country west of Lake Rudolf, Kenya

Primitive Peoples of Africa

THROUGH the work of the explorers, the missionaries, and now the modern businessmen and representatives of foreign governments, most of Africa has been influenced by white people in one way or another.

There are still some people like the Bushmen, however, whose tribal life remains much as it has been for centuries. These untouched people were formerly called "savages," but today we use the word "primitives"; the word points out that although their civilization is not modern, they nevertheless do have a civilization of their own. Often their basic ways of living are more suited to the climate and the conditions under which they exist than European

Native dancers of Ruanda-Urundi, East Africa

A leader of the Suk tribe, Kenya

ways are. When white customs are introduced, the primitive peoples
sometimes do not fare well. Tribal laws go to pieces, for certain
parts of white civilization do the people more harm than good. But
there is no stopping the changes that are taking place in Africa. It is
a land that is rapidly passing from one stage of development to another. Before the end of the twentieth century there may no longer
be any truly primitive peoples left on the continent.

Primitive government in Africa usually began with the clan, a
group of blood relatives who formed a cluster of villages. As the
clan grew, people were less and less directly related through family
ties but still had a common language and common customs; the tribe
came into being. A tribe may inhabit many hundreds of square miles
and have many villages within its area. Usually the ruler is a chief.
Often the chieftainship is handed down from father to son, but on
the other hand a chief may simply be the strongest or wisest man in

A woman of Basutoland

the tribe or a man chosen by a council of elders. Some tribes have a queen, but usually a male rules and the older and wiser men of the tribe help him to make decisions.

Land usually belongs to the tribe as a whole, but is parceled out to families for farming. Women do most of the planting and sowing of crops, and sell at the market the produce they do not need. Women also cook, weave, and tend the children. Primitive men usually hunt and fish, killing game for food. Men herd the cattle, clear the land, and build the houses. They protect the villages from wild animals; if there is a war, men are the fighters.

In many African tribes a man may marry more than one wife. There are practical reasons for this. The more women there are in a family, the more help there is for tending the gardens and fields. Moreover, the more sons a man has, the more protection he and his village will have in time of war. Men take pride in many wives and

Fishing in the Kivu area of the Congo

The Stick Dance of the Amakwenke tribesmen

large families. All are members of the tribe and no one is neglected or goes hungry. Brides are usually purchased from their parents, or a dowry of cattle, grain, or money is given to the girl's family. In some tribes, women take part in making important decisions, but in others they have no word of authority except in the household.

Primitive Africans respect many gods. In some tribes like the Yoruba of Nigeria there are more than four hundred deities. Often each god represents some part of nature, such as water, thunder, lightning, or the sun. There may also be a god of war, of love, of planting, or of the harvest. In English, primitive priests are often called "witch doctors" or "medicine men" for, besides calling on the powers of the various gods, they work to cure illnesses. Primitive people often think a cure is made by the casting out of the evil spirits that cause sickness.

Almost all ceremonies in tribal life are in some way related to the gods, and drums and music play a great part in primitive religions. The gods are called on by music to bless the planting and the har-

A Congo tribesman sending a message by drum

Native village of Togoland

vest, or to make successful a hunting expedition — or to receive
thanks when a son is born. Drums are also used in trials of wrong-
doers, to emphasize a chief's judgments; in warfare they excite men
to a fighting pitch; on happy occasions they are used for dancing.
Drums may still carry messages from one village to another in some
places. Faster than a man can talk, drumbeats can tell of a missionary approaching up the river, of a lion in the vicinity, or of danger
from a neighboring enemy tribe.

Even the most primitive of the Africans, as Livingstone discovered, are not savage in the animal sense, nor are they dangerous to
strangers unless they are angered or harmed. Many tribes are most

33

Building a hut in Togoland

kindly to travelers passing through their villages. A recent American writer has said that today it is possible for a white man to travel from one end of Africa to the other without danger from the natives. Most wild animals in Africa will also leave men alone, if men have not frightened or disturbed them. Human beings had best watch out for snakes and crocodiles, however, for they attack without warning.

Home Life and Arts in Primitive Africa

PRIMITIVE men seldom live apart from one another. They usually dwell in villages, and sometimes their huts are grouped around a central clearing. The huts are often built of stout poles, roofed with palm thatch or mats of tightly woven grass. Some tribes use a mud-like brick for building, and others a kind of adobe plaster over a framework of woven twigs. There are tribes whose huts of mud and straw are shaped like beehives, and other tribes whose homes are rounded, like igloos. Usually African homes are very clean — swept often, and with little or no furniture except mats spread on dirt floors. Cooking is usually done over outdoor fireplaces, and washing is carried to the nearest lake or creek, where baths are taken, too. Festivals are held outdoors.

A small Mangbettu drum

A ceremonial hornblower of the Chagga tribe

Carved wooden pillars or statues dedicated to one's ancestors may decorate homes or shrines, but usually African art is not "art for art's sake." Rather, it is art applied to useful objects: a beautiful carved cup of wood or ivory in the shape of a head, a decorated bowl or spoon, a hand-carved chair or stool, a shield for hunting or for war, a handle for a spear, or a mask for a religious ceremony. Art like the great Benin heads of bronze and other similar ancient objects is not being created in Africa today. Yet, in areas seldom touched by European traders with their factory-made articles, hand-made objects that are both useful and lovely to look at are still being produced.

African music and its rhythms came across the seas to the West Indies and the Americas three hundred years ago, and in the United

36

States helped to make jazz. The same ancient rhythms may be heard in many parts of Africa today. Drums of varying tones are the basic instruments, but there are other percussion instruments such as gourds, rattles, sticks, and stamping-tubes of bamboo. Various kinds of reeds and flutes are played, also. A small flat frame crossed by strips of metal or bamboo is in common use; it is played with the thumbs and is called a "sansa" or "thumb piano." The Watusi of Ruanda play large stringed harps. The Bapende of the Congo have long xylophones, wooden slabs mounted on a set of hollow gourds and played with sticks that have gummed heads. They make beautiful melodies. Music-making, singing, and dancing are favorite pastimes with Africans everywhere.

Africans love to tell stories, riddles, and proverbs, too. There is much wisdom in a Ewe proverb that says, "Until you have crossed the river, never tease a crocodile." Another proverb from the same people advises, "An animal with a long tail should not try to jump over a fire." And from the Kru people: "A dog says, 'I have never called a man to come to me and then beaten him.'"

Each African tribe usually has one or more official storytellers, usually old men who act as tribal historians also. Since primitive peoples have no books, all the history of a tribe must be handed down by memory from one generation to another. Early in life young men are chosen to learn from older storytellers all that has happened to their ancestors. These men are the "human books" of tribal lore and wisdom. Aside from being teachers they often tell stories around an outdoor fire at night, just for fun. Sometimes the stories try to explain *why* things are, as this tale from the Ibibio tribe in Nigeria does.

MANY YEARS AGO *the Sun and the Water were great friends, and* both lived on the earth together. The Sun very often used to visit the Water, but the Water never returned his visits. At last the Sun asked the Water why it was that he never came to see him in his house. The Water replied that the Sun's house was not big enough, and that if ever he came with all his people they would drive the Sun out.

The Water said, "If you wish me to visit you, you must build a very large yard — but I warn you that it will have to be a tremendous place, as my people are very numerous and take up a lot of room."

The Sun promised to build a very big yard. Soon afterward he returned home to his wife, the Moon, who greeted him with a broad smile when he opened the door. The Sun told the Moon what he had promised the Water, and the next day he started building a huge yard in which to entertain his friend. When it was completed, he asked the Water to come and visit him. When the Water arrived, he called out to the Sun and asked him whether it would be safe to enter.

The Sun answered, "Yes. Come in, my friend."

The Water began to flow in, accompanied by the fish and all the other water animals. Very soon the Water was knee-deep, so he asked the Sun if it was still safe.

The Sun said, "Yes."

At that, more water creatures came in.

When the Water was level with the top of a man's head, the Water said to the Sun, "Do you want more of my people to come?"

The Sun and the Moon both answered, "Yes," not knowing any better.

Water continued to flow until the Sun and the Moon had to perch on the top of the roof. Again the Water addressed the Sun. And again he received the same answer. More of his people rushed in.

38

Very soon the Water overflowed the top of the roof. Then the Sun and the Moon were forced to go up into the sky, where they have remained ever since.

And that is why they are so far above the earth.

Children of Africa

THE children of primitive Africa are seldom separated from their elders. They listen to their stories at night, and work or play beside the older folk in the daytime. Early in life, children are given little tasks to do, and they gradually grow into the work habits of the tribe. The boys herd cattle, aid in clearing the fields, or go with the men on hunting or fishing trips. The girls help tend the huts and sweep the village yards. Usually the girls and women cultivate the village gardens in which maize, beans, cassava, and peppers are grown. Children dig for peanuts (called groundnuts in Africa) and pick papaws, mangoes, bananas, and coconuts.

But there is plenty of playtime, too, and African children have their own games, many of them somewhat like American games. The children learn to make drums and flutes, to sing and dance, and to repeat riddles and stories. In most tribes, when boys and girls approach their teens they go through ceremonies that teach them the things they will need to know as grownups. These ceremonies are different from tribe to tribe, but usually the boys spend a time apart in the forest where they are tested for their bravery and their readiness to become strong men. The girls may live in huts apart from others for weeks, too, while they are advised by older women of the tribe as to the duties of wives and mothers. Great feasts and dances are usually held when the time comes for bringing the young people into the tribe as grown-up members.

39

A young Chagga girl

In most of the large cities of Africa, however, tribal customs are disappearing, and life for children is now much the same as it is in other lands. The old ways are being forgotten under the influence of missionary education and European ways of living. Today there are Boy Scouts in the Congo, and many students in Cape Town study Latin. In recent years young African delegates have attended international high school forums in New York City. And, although the number is not yet large, more and more young Africans are going to Europe or the United States for college education.

Changing Africa

Not only in the cities, but over most of Africa the coming of the Europeans has brought many changes. Mining and the starting of

Road repairing in the village of Kumba, Cameroons

industries have made new kinds of work. Natives in remote villages are meeting Europeans, and some of the tribesmen have been educated by missionaries. Western clothes and western habits are being introduced even to some lonely settlements. American jazz is in some places beginning to have an influence on African tribal music. Roads have been built, and motor cars imported; as a result, men can now travel in an hour the same distances that once took days. Airplanes make it possible for African leaders and chiefs to attend meetings in cities like Accra or Cairo; they can come from their far-off countries within a day, whereas it would formerly have taken weeks, perhaps even months, to make so long a journey. Messages once relayed overland by the beat of drums may now be sent by telegraph or radio. The changes on their continent have been so

Music rehearsal at an African school in Tanganyika

A Pokoma hospital assistant going to work among his people, Kenya

great that now the Africans can never go back to their former ways.

Part of the changes that the Europeans have brought to some areas have been good — things such as education, better health arrangements in large cities, the possible end of slave trading, and in some places, a chance to see how a democratic government works.

Not all the changes have been good, however. At first, the white newcomers did not understand tribal customs and they tried to do away with them in many areas. Or they tried to change African ways too quickly. The new methods brought about great confusion, upset the old, time-tried ways of doing things, and caused many Africans to hate Europeans.

Then, too, when the white settlers made the mining of gold, diamonds, and uranium into great industries, Africans were lured away from their tribes into the mines. They were also offered work in the homes, shops, and factories of great cities like Johannesburg, in South Africa. In recent years some forty millions of natives have left their tribal villages and their families behind them to work in European centers and industries. But they have not been given the same rights or wages as white workers. The unfair treatment they

Adult education class in a native village, Cameroons

have received and the breakdown of the old tribal customs have made serious problems for everyone.

Now the ugly situations that the coming of the Europeans created need to be settled. What happens in Africa is bound up today with the affairs not only of Europe but of the United States as well. If answers for Africa's problems are not found, the peace of the whole world may be upset.

But what are the answers? What will take the place of the old tribal customs that are disappearing? How quickly can an African tribesman become used to modern civilization, and what happens

Native gold miners more than 7,000 feet underground, South Africa

Change of shift in a Nigerian coal mine

when he does? How can the Africans best take their place in the modern world, and how can they be sure of fair treatment under new conditions?

Searching for ways to solve their problems, the various African people feel the need to control their own governments. Let's look at some of Africa's modern governments.

Africa's Governments

AFRICA has ten completely independent countries: Cameroun, Egypt, Ethiopia (also called Abyssinia), Libya, Liberia, Morocco, the Sudan, Togoland, Tunisia, and the Republic of Guinea. Here the countries govern themselves. The oldest of the independent nations in Africa are Ethiopia and Egypt; their histories go back many centuries, and during this time they have been independent except for brief periods. Ethiopia is a kingdom, ruled by an emperor. Egypt is now a republic, although it has not always been one. Liberia, however, is the oldest republic in Africa, dating its formation from 1847. Among the new completely independent nations of Africa are the United Kingdom of Libya, formed in 1952; the Republic of the Sudan, the Republic of Tunisia, and the Kingdom of Morocco, all of which achieved independence in 1956; the Republic of Guinea, formed in 1958; and Cameroun and Togoland, independent early in 1960.

The Union of South Africa and the new state of Ghana, as free members of the British Commonwealth, have like Canada only slight ties to the British Empire.

Aside from these twelve countries all the other lands of Africa were, early in 1960, a part of the colonial world, and had ties with governments outside the African continent.

Ways of running the government, and the treatment of the native peoples, varied widely from country to country — even in different countries under the same European ruler. For example, the native peoples of Nigeria, under the British, had much more political freedom than the natives of Kenya. As a result, Nigeria went through a peaceful change toward statehood, whereas Kenya experienced a dangerous native revolt against the British government.

In French Algeria there was unrest and rebellion, but in French West Africa there was peace. The formerly French Guinea, like the formerly British Ghana, was freely building its own future.

Kenya: A Trouble Spot

In contrast to Ghana and Nigeria, where the future looks hopeful, Kenya is an unhappy land where whites fear blacks and blacks hate whites. Yet Kenya, too, is a part of the British Empire. Its strip of

Kibo Peak, Mount Kilimanjaro, Tanganyika

Nyali Beach, near Mombasa, Kenya

coast is a protectorate, and the rest of Kenya is a crown colony. This country, lying on the equator between Ethiopia and Tanganyika, runs from the Indian Ocean to Lake Victoria and the borders of Uganda. Its climate ranges from temperate in the high plateaus to hot and humid in the lowlands, and its scenery is as varied as its climate. There is snow at the top of 17,040-foot Mount Kenya, yet

49

Giraffes in their native surroundings

Lionesses on a game reserve, Nairobi, Kenya

Lion on a game reserve, Nairobi, Kenya

Cutting sisal on a Tanganyika plantation

along the coast regal palms and brilliant tropical flowers grow.
Kenya's railroad, built largely by East Indian labor, runs from Lake
Victoria to the sea through one of the most exciting big-game areas
in the world. From the train windows a passenger may sometimes
see not only untamed lions, but enormous elephants, tall giraffes,
and graceful gazelles.

Kenya has a population of about six millions of people, yet only about sixty thousand, or 1 per cent of them, are white. The whites, however, rule the country and have taken possession of almost all the best land.

Most of the British live on the high plateaus where the climate is cool, much as it is in England. They have staked out large farms and cattle-grazing meadows on land taken from the Africans. This area, called the White Highlands, is so productive that there are two harvests a year. Only white men may own land here. All that is left to the native tribes are the most arid and hard-to-cultivate areas, known as reserves — and the natives may even be moved from this land without notice or without their consent. The largest tribes are the Kikuyu, the Kamba, and the Masai. Many of their members leave the overcrowded reserves to work under a sort of plantation system for British farmers whose chief products are coffee, tea, sisal, and grain.

Spraying coffee trees on a Kenya plantation

Kikuyu woman, Kenya

But even so, about a million of the Kikuyus of the region have been crowded into some two thousand square miles of unfertile land, although less than four thousand whites occupy sixteen thousand square miles.

Seeking to get some of their land back, the Kikuyus took up arms against the British settlers and through their secret society the Mau Mau began a campaign of death and terror. In 1954 the Mau Mau were crushed by the military might of the whites, and were arrested in masses and confined to reserves. They are no longer openly active, but the natives still feel a smoldering hatred and the white farmers must sleep with guns beside their beds.

Some way will have to be found in the future for the natives to have a share of Kenya's good things. But most of the whites in Kenya do not wish to grant the Africans land, education, or political equality. In public places the color line is strictly drawn. In Nairobi, the capital, neither Africans nor East Indians are admitted to the hotels, cafes, or clubs of the white people. The situation is not a happy one, but in the Commonwealth of South Africa conditions are even worse for people of color.

South Africa: Land of Apartheid

SOUTH AFRICA has the largest white population of any country on the continent — about three million, almost evenly divided between those of Dutch and those of British descent. But people of color far outnumber the whites. The country has nearly ten million Africans, a million and one-half people of mixed blood, and a half million Indians and Malayans. Yet South Africa has stricter laws against people of color than any other country in the world. Under its system of "white supremacy," called *apartheid* (pronounced a-PART-hate), black Africans may not vote, attend schools with whites, or travel without a pass. There are separate living areas in the cities, separate buses, and separate railway cars for persons of color. Forced labor exists, and the workers in the gold and diamond mines are treated almost like slaves. Even missionaries are hindered in their work in churches and schools. Those who protest against these unfair conditions are arrested for "treason," whether they are black or white.

The Union of South Africa has a British governor general, but the country is actually run by its own parliament, a premier, and his cabinet. The administrative center is at Pretoria, while the seat of the parliament is at Cape Town. The descendants of the Dutch, called Boers or Afrikaners, have the balance of power in the government and, because for years they fought against the Bantu tribes in the old days, they now oppose any advancement for the natives or East Indians.

The climate of South Africa is temperate; there is summer and winter as in Europe; and there are fine beaches and high mountains. The largest city, Johannesburg, is more than a mile high, on the Witwatersrand, a ridge where gold was discovered in 1886. There are skyscrapers in Johannesburg, and beautiful theaters and parks — for whites only. Other fine South African cities are Cape Town, at the foot of Table Mountain; Durban, with miles of sandy beaches on the Indian Ocean; and Kimberley, where the deepest man-made hole on earth is located, created by the diamond-mining operations. In the Transvaal there are lovely old Dutch towns surrounded by

View of Capetown, South Africa

Premier Diamond Mine near Pretoria, South Africa

orchards and vineyards. And the world's largest sanctuary for wild animals is Kruger National Park near the border of Mozambique.

South Africa has a high intellectual level compared to the rest of the continent. Famous writers like Alan Paton, white man who wrote *Cry, the Beloved Country*, and Peter Abrahams, colored man who wrote *Tell Freedom*, are South Africans. In Johannesburg the largest magazine for African readers, *Drum*, is published, with writers and editors of color on its staff. Nevertheless, as regards fair rights for all races, South Africa, like Kenya, is most backward. New and even harsher laws have lately been passed to keep the native peoples from advancing any further in education or politics. Although all of the South African mines and industries depend on native labor for their output, the natives themselves are not permitted to share in any of the benefits of their country's wealth.

And, with its diamonds, uranium, and gold, the Union of South Africa has great wealth; it is the most advanced country on the continent — for Europeans. It produces more than a million tons of steel a year. Its cities are the largest and most modern. It has excellent universities. But for the native peoples it is, with Kenya, the worst place to live — and even educated natives are seldom permitted to travel outside the country. The South African system of white supremacy permits persons of color almost no freedom at all, therefore today they are in a state of half-rebellion which newspapermen predict is likely to burst into violence at any time.

Belgian Congo: Troubled Colonialism

NEXT to the Union of South Africa, the most industrialized region on the continent is the Belgian Congo. It has over 900,000 square miles of land, is nearly eighty times the size of the European country that controlled it for many years, and has a population more than a third greater than that of Belgium itself. It has the tallest people in the world, the Watusi; one of the longest rivers in the world, the Congo; and the largest uranium mine on earth, Shinkolobwe. The material to produce the first atom bomb came from this mine, and the United States is still Shinkolobwe's leading customer.

The Belgian Congo is the world's largest source of industrial diamonds. Gold, tin, copper, cobalt, used in jet engines, germanium, used in transistors, and manganese also add to its enormous mineral wealth. Palm oil and hardwoods are a part of its riches. Exports amount to more than $3,000,000,000 a year. Belgium is a great European power because of what it has taken from the Congo.

In recent years the Belgians have hoped to keep the African mine and foundry workers happy by making their living conditions as good as possible. In the cities modern housing, hospitals, and missionary schools have been built for the natives brought from their tribal areas to the mines and industrial districts. In the native quarters of the larger cities more new housing, bright movie houses, and good restaurants were to be found than in any other part of colonial Africa. To keep away mosquitoes, helicopters sprayed entire cities regularly. Belgian foremen and officials even went to the trouble of learning tribal languages, a task which few whites bothered with in other colonies. Africans themselves held many office jobs, acted as customs officers, tax collectors, and postal clerks, and worked at skilled and semi-skilled labor. But the races have been kept strictly apart. In Léopoldville, capital of the Congo, Europeans and Africans live in separate sections. Colored peoples have been made to carry passes permitting them to walk about the city, and for them there has been a nine o'clock curfew after which they could not be seen in white districts.

Nobody in the Congo, white or black, has voted in the past. Whites have occupied all the top positions, and the government has been directed from Brussels, in Belgium. Many native Africans in the Belgian Congo wanted to vote, and wished to have a say in running the affairs of their land. Like the New England colonists in the 1770's, who grew tired of British control, so the Congolese finally asked for reforms. But the Belgians then took away their right to hold meetings, banned African papers and political parties, and put native leaders in prison. In 1959 riots broke out in Léopoldville, Matadi, and other cities. Police and soldiers fired on the natives, and almost two hundred were reported killed. Many others were imprisoned.

In all the Belgian Congo there are only about 125,000 whites, as compared to 13,000,000 blacks. The National Congolese Movement, under the leadership of native Africans who up to 1960 had no part at all in their own government, has stated that it aims finally to obtain the freedoms guaranteed by the United Nations Charter, and to obtain, through discussion and after a reasonable time, the independence of the Congo. Africans feel that when they first asked for discussions of the subject they should not have been arrested, met by police with armored cars, and forbidden to hold public meetings. There is now a troubled peace between the Europeans and the Africans in the Congo. But there is a feeling of hope, too. The Belgian King Baudoin has made the first official promise of independence to the people. An early date has been set, and everyone waits to see what this promise will achieve.

Guinea: Freedom by Ballot

JUST across the river from the Belgian Congo lies the vast territory of Equatorial Africa. It stretches away, northward and westward around Nigeria, to join with West Africa. This French community of nations has an enormous number of natives — about 25 millions of them. In Paris, in 1958, the French Premier Charles de Gaulle offered his African territories the right to make a choice by voting. They were to choose between being completely independent or remaining within the French Overseas Community, either as a part of France or as a country with local self-government.

Waiting to vote in Togoland

Several of the colonies chose to remain in the French Overseas Community as semi-independent republics. These include Mauritania, Chad, Gabon, the Congo Republic, the Malagasy Republic (formerly Madagascar), Dahomey, and Senegal, now joined with the French Sudan into the Mali Federation. Only Guinea chose to separate itself completely from France and form an independent republic under the leadership of Sékou Touré, who became its first African premier. There were no violent uprisings or long-drawn-out conferences. Guinea took de Gaulle at his word and simply voted to be free.

Many people predicted that the country would have a difficult time in governing itself — particularly in obtaining enough money. But Sékou Touré said, "We prefer poverty in liberty to riches in slavery." He immediately set about trying to make his country's trade, industry, and banking secure. Shortly after freedom, Guinea joined with Ghana to form a union which both states hope will in time lead to a sort of "United States of Africa."

Guinea is located on the West Coast just north of Sierra Leone. It has a population of over two and a half million; its area is 105,200 square miles; and it has rich deposits of iron ore, bauxite (used in the making of aluminum), and diamonds. This buried wealth, as yet only partly mined, now produces more than $5,000,000 a year in export value. But most of Guinea's laborers work on plantations, raising coffee, bananas, oranges, peanuts, pineapples, and palm oil. Rubber plantations also bring in money. France still carries on business and banking in Guinea, and Frenchmen are still big investors there, but the people of Guinea now control their own government.

Liberia: Godchild of the U.S.A.

LIBERIA is a child of American freedom. In 1822 the land it occupies was purchased by the American Colonization Society as a haven for freed slaves; twenty-five years later Liberia became a republic. Its government was modeled after that of the United States. Its flag is red, white, and blue, but has only a single star. Like the United States, Liberia has a Congress of both senators and representatives, and a Cabinet selected by the President. All its citizens who own property or pay hut-taxes may vote, women as well as men. The President is head of the military forces.

Liberia lies just north of the equator on the Atlantic Ocean. Its climate is humid, with a heavy rainfall, and much of the land is covered with tropical jungles. It is one of the smallest countries in Africa, being only about the size of Pennsylvania. Its population is probably less than three millions of persons, who are either the descendants of the freed slaves who settled there, called Americo-Liberians, or members of twenty-three native tribes. The largest of the tribes are the Mandingo, Kru, Bassa, Grebo, and Vai. Long before outsiders brought the English alphabet, the Vai had a written language, one of three in all of primitive Africa. And the Krumen were an enlightened people, great fishermen and seamen, many of whom now work on foreign ships during voyages up and down the African West Coast.

Most of the people are very poor, but under President William V. S. Tubman the country has increased its income enormously, largely with the aid of such American investors as the Firestone Tire and Rubber Company and the Liberian Mining Company. Each year Liberia now exports enough rubber to make tires for almost half the cars manufactured in the United States. Besides that, it exports over a million tons of the world's richest iron ore, and much cocoa and palm oil.

Liberia was long neglected by the land that created it, but America has now begun to take a new official interest in it. Through the Point Four program, a plan for giving technical aid, the government of the United States today contributes more than $1,000,000 a year to Liberia. A number of experts trained in agriculture, public health, education, and other fields have been sent from America to help the country. The capital and port of Monrovia, named after United States President James Monroe, has been made larger and brought up to date by American engineers, who have also built a large airport and an American military base at Roberts Field and have designed a system of highways. President Tubman has paid an official visit to the White House, and numbers of Liberian students now come to the United States for higher education. Today there are many American technicians, teachers, and missionaries living in Liberia. The country remains all-Negro, however, in that persons of other races may not become citizens or purchase land, although they are welcomed as investors, technicians, teachers, and advisers.

Ghana: A Free Commonwealth

ONE of the most interesting African republics is Ghana, which in 1957 was made a member of the British Commonwealth. Ghana was formerly the territory of British Togoland and the Gold Coast; it took its new name from the ancient African kingdom whose center was Timbuktu. Its first premier, Kwame Nkrumah, was educated at Lincoln University in Pennsylvania, and later lived in London.

Though many of its people are poor, Ghana is a wealthy country, well able to support itself. It exports two-thirds of the world's cocoa

Fishermen, Ghana

and has the largest supply of bauxite ore on earth. There are also
diamonds in Ghana, besides gold, manganese, and great forests of
hardwood. Accra, its capital, is a city on the Gulf of Guinea, where
once slave ships plied their trade.

The population of Ghana is about five million. In proportion to
the number of its inhabitants this new republic has more children in
school than any other land in Africa. For the future, the people of
Ghana have great plans for improving their country. They plan to
dam the Volta River, then build one of the largest hydroelectric

plants in the world. They also intend to erect on the banks of the Volta a plant to make aluminum of the bauxite deposits along the river. The project will give low-cost electrical power and lighting to a large area of the country.

In Ghana all grownups can vote. The country is governed by a parliament, and the whole plan of government and courts is like that of England. Kwame Nkrumah, Ghana's first prime minister, also founded the leading political group, the Convention People's Party, in 1949. Most other political parties in the country have banded together into a single opposition force called the United Party. But there are important tribal chiefs who still have the power to act as tyrants. Nkrumah must bring these chiefs into line with the democracy he is trying to form. Yet at the same time he must try to allow those who do not agree with him the right to criticize and oppose him freely. This is a problem, for a new democracy.

Since Ghana's independence, foreign investments and advisers are welcomed. Many white English judges and civil servants have been kept in their former positions, and white people continue to live and work in Ghana without harm. Nkrumah does not hold a grudge against the British who once, he feels, ruled his country unjustly. In his public speeches he has stated that there should be "an absence of the desire for vengeance for our wrongs . . . in a world sick of injustice, revenge, fear, and want." And he has said this about independence: "Self-government is not an end in itself. It is a means to an end, to the building of the good life for the benefit of all."

Today the eyes of the world are on Ghana because in that country is a test whether native Africans can make a success of self-government. Ghana has many different tribes speaking forty-six languages within its borders, and it has believers of many different religions. The uniting of so many varied peoples into a common

66

democracy is not easy. But Prime Minister Nkrumah is a very able man, and other natives high in the government are capable, too.

The people have given Nkrumah the nickname of "Show Boy." This name means that they are proud of him and like to show off his abilities to the rest of the world. The black peoples of Africa and the forward-looking white residents on the continent hope Ghana will succeed in becoming a successful modern state. But some white colonizers in Kenya or South Africa hope that Ghana will fail and thus discourage further efforts at freedom on the continent. They are fearful that someone like "Show Boy" may gain popular favor with the natives in their countries. These white people aim to keep all the governing power in the hands of Europeans and to allow the Africans no political rights at all. What happens to Ghana in the near future will influence the history of all Africa.

Harvesting cocoa pods, Ghana

The U. S. A., the U. N., and Africa

THE United States, through its Point Four program, gives teaching and technical assistance to a number of African countries besides Liberia. With the building of demonstration houses from a new type of sun-baked brick in Egypt, the killing of swarms of crop-eating locusts in Ethiopia, and many other activities American experts have brought Africa a practical kind of assistance that was not known before. The Point Four Visual Aids program has introduced new educational methods to African teachers. And, of course, the United States contributes both money and workers to such United Nations organizations as UNESCO (United Nations Educational, Scientific and Cultural Organization) and the World Health Organization; their work is of great value in colonial countries. All the free nations of Africa are members of the United Nations. But the Union of South Africa has recently been at odds with the United Nations over the South African "apartheid" policy of extreme color discrimination, which is directly contrary to the ideas put forth in the United Nations covenant. With representatives of black Africa now taking part in United Nations councils, the problems of colonial rule and the color bar are bound to become more and more a part of United Nations discussions.

Africa Tomorrow

THE eyes of the world are upon the "trouble spots" of Africa. Among the troubled areas are Algeria, where the native peoples no longer wish to be a part of France, Kenya, South Africa, and the Rhodesias, where the governments show great injustice to the colored races. Meanwhile, Nigeria's independence within the British Commonwealth of Nations will give that country a chance to develop a democracy. If Ghana successfully weathers the early years of its new self-government, more and more of the African colonial states will become impatient to have independence. Most authorities on Africa today agree that terrible violence can be avoided only by paving the way for such independence.

"For better or for worse the old Africa is gone and the white races must face the new situation which they have themselves created," said Jan Christian Smuts, the white South African leader, before his death.

"Our struggle is simple: it is for political freedom, economic opportunity, and human dignity for all Africans," says the young black chairman of the first All-African People's Conference, Tom Mboya. "We want in our countries to have the right to self-determination, to have a government elected by our people, responsible to our people, and accountable to our people."

The new leaders of black Africa like Mboya of Kenya, Touré of Guinea, Nkrumah of Ghana, and Azikiwe of Nigeria know that independence brings problems. They know that many African regions just freeing themselves from foreign government will need to be guided as they take their first steps toward independence. They realize that their people cannot get along without work, food, and money. They will need investments and practical help from other countries, to develop fully the rich natural resources of Africa. They ask the other nations of the world to be patient with them.

Africa's leaders of color today are aware of the many tribal and religious differences on their vast continent, where about one-fourth of the population is Moslem, one-tenth Christian, and the rest worship various gods, and where there is great variety in languages and

ways of living. They know that four-fifths of Africa's enormous population cannot read or write, and that most are unfamiliar with modern machinery.

But Africa's leaders know that the natives can learn to read and write, as the people of Ghana are doing. In the Congo the leaders have seen that Africans can operate complicated machinery or become skillful in industrial laboratories. And they believe that Africans can govern themselves, as they have been doing for generations in those countries that did not come under colonial rule.

Although mistakes may be made at first, African leaders feel that people can learn to govern only by practicing government. For the sake of their own dignity, they must have the opportunity to try. Leaders admit that there are difficulties to be faced in independence. When Nkrumah says, however, "We prefer self-government with danger to servitude in tranquillity," he is expressing the feeling of most of the people of black Africa today.

It is a world-wide aim that people of all races should be able to live together in peace and freedom. May that aim be reached in the future of Africa, a country whose earth is rich, whose landscape is beautiful and varied, and whose native peoples eagerly seek a better life as they step forward into the modern world. For a very long time white Europeans ruled Africa, and many Europeans will wish to continue to live in the Africa of future days. Concerning them and their responsibilities toward the new Africa the great South African writer, Alan Paton, has written: "They brought a new life to this country. They changed the old life beyond recall. It goes on changing, and it is our duty to see that it changes for the good of all who live here. . . . Justice in the ideal is a powerful thing, but justice in practice is more powerful still, and can influence powerfully all the peoples of the world."

70

Students are preparing to take their place in the new Africa

The Countries of Africa

(Since in many areas no complete census has ever been taken, the population figures for some countries can only be estimated.)

COUNTRY	AREA [SQ. MI.]	POPULATION	CAPITAL
Independent			
Cameroun (REPUBLIC)	166,489	3,187,000	Yaoundé
Egypt (REPUBLIC)	386,198	23,410,000	Cairo
Ethiopia (KINGDOM)	350,000	19,500,000	Addis Ababa
Guinea (REPUBLIC)	105,200	2,505,000	Conakry
Liberia (REPUBLIC)	43,000	2,750,000	Monrovia
Libya (KINGDOM)	679,358	1,091,830	Tripoli and Bengazi
Morocco (KINGDOM)	172,104	9,823,000	Rabat
The Sudan (REPUBLIC)	967,500	10,000,000	Khartoum
Togoland (REPUBLIC)	21,893	1,088,000	Lomé
Tunisia (REPUBLIC)	48,313	3,800,000	Tunis
Independent Members British Commonwealth			
Ghana	91,843	4,763,000	Accra
Union of South Africa	472,550	14,418,000	Pretoria and Cape Town

COUNTRY	AREA [SQ. MI.]	POPULATION	CAPITAL
British Colonies or Protectorates			
Basutoland	11,716	634,000	Maseru
Bechuanaland	294,020	327,000	Mafeking
Central African Federation			
Northern Rhodesia	290,323	2,180,000	Lusaka
Southern Rhodesia	150,333	2,480,000	Salisbury
Nyasaland	47,404	3,266,000	Zomba
Gambia	4,005	311,000	Bathurst
Kenya	224,960	6,261,000	Nairobi
Mauritius and dependencies	720	596,857	Port Louis
Nigeria (Independence in 1960)	373,250	34,700,000	Lagos
St. Helena and dependencies	119	5,355	Jamestown
Seychelles	156	40,417	Victoria
Sierra Leone	27,925	2,500,000	Freetown
Somaliland	68,000	640,000	Hargeisa
South-West Africa	317,887	458,000	Windhoek
Swaziland	6,704	241,000	Mbabane
Tanganyika Territory (U.N. Trusteeship)	362,688	8,452,619	Dar es Salaam
Uganda	93,981	5,680,000	Entebbe and Kampala
Zanzibar and Pamba	1,020	285,000	Zanzibar
French Colonies or Protectorates			
Algeria	852,600	9,530,500	Algiers
Central African Republic (Ubangi-Shari)	238,000	1,121,000	Bangui
Chad Republic	496,000	2,521,000	Fort-Lamy
Comoro Archipelago	790	180,000	Pamanzi
Congo Republic	132,000	745,000	Pointe Noire
Dahomey Republic	45,900	1,614,000	Porto-Novo
French Somaliland	9,071	65,403	Jibuti

74

COUNTRY	AREA [SQ. MI.]	POPULATION	CAPITAL
Gabon Republic	103,000	420,000	Libreville
Ivory Coast Republic	123,200	2,481,000	Abidjan
Malagasy Republic (Madagascar and dependencies)	241,094	4,913,000	Tananarive
Mali Federation			
French Sudan	450,000	3,346,900	Bamako
Senegal	80,600	2,220,000	St. Louis
Mauritania	415,900	615,000	St. Louis (Senegal)
Niger Republic	494,500	2,334,000	Niamey
Réunion	969	274,370	St. Denis
Upper Voltiac Republic	105,900	3,324,000	Ouagadougou

Belgian Colonies and U.N. Trust Territory

Congo (Independence promised in 1960)	904,757	12,660,000	Léopoldville
Ruanda-Urundi (Trust territory)	20,742	4,424,573	Usumbura

Portuguese Colonies

Angola	481,351	4,354,000	Luanda
Cape Verde Islands	1,557	166,000	Praia
Mozambique	297,731	6,170,000	Lourenço Marques
Portuguese Guinea	13,948	554,000	Bissau
São Tomé-Principe	372	53,000	Santo Antonio

Spanish Colonies

Ifni	740	38,000	Sidi Ifni
Spanish Guinea	10,852	212,000	Santa Isabel
Spanish Sahara			
Rio de Oro	73,362	23,000	Villa Cisneros
Sekia el Hamra	32,047	10,000	Smara

COUNTRY	AREA [SQ. MI.]	POPULATION	CAPITAL
Italian U.N. Trust Territory			
Somalia (Trusteeship ending 1960)	194,000	1,255,000	Mogadiscio

Index

77

Picture Credits

82